OUR LIVING WORLD

Fungi

By **Jenny Tesar**

With Illustrations by Wendy Smith-Griswold

Series Editor: Vincent Marteka
Introduction by John Behler, *New York Zoological Society*

A BLACKBIRCH PRESS BOOK
WOODBRIDGE, CONNECTICUT

Published by Blackbirch Press, Inc.
One Bradley Road, Suite 205
Woodbridge, CT 06525

©1994 Blackbirch Press, Inc.
First Edition

Printed in Canada

10 9 8 7 6 5 4 3 2 1

Editorial Director: Bruce Glassman
Editor: Tanya Lee Stone
Assistant Editor: Elizabeth M. Taylor
Design Director: Sonja Kalter
Production: Sandra Burr, Rudy Raccio, Madeline Parker

Library of Congress Cataloging-in-Publication Data

Tesar, Jenny E.
    Fungi / by Jenny Tesar; with illustrations by Wendy Smith-Griswold—1st ed.
        p.   cm. — (Our living world)
    Includes bibliographical references and index.
    ISBN 1-56711-044-4
    1. Fungi—Juvenile literature. [1. Fungi.] I. Smith-Griswold, Wendy, ill.
II. Title. III. Series.
QK603.5.T47 1994
589.2—dc20   93-44542
                                                                          CIP
                                                                          AC

Contents

What Does It Mean to Be "Alive"?

Introduction by John Behler,
New York Zoological Society

One summer morning, as I was walking through a beautiful field, I was inspired to think about what it really means to be "alive." Part of the answer, I came to realize, was right in front of my eyes.

The meadow was ablaze with color, packed with wildflowers at the height of their blooming season. A multitude of insects, warmed by the sun's early-morning rays, began to stir. Painted turtles sunned themselves on an old mossy log in a nearby pond. A pair of wood ducks whistled a call as they flew overhead, resting near a shagbark hickory on the other side of the pond.

As I wandered through this unspoiled habitat, I paused at a patch of milkweed to look for monarch-butterfly caterpillars, which depend on the milkweed's leaves for food. Indeed, the caterpillars were there, munching away. Soon these larvae would spin their cocoons, emerge as beautiful orange-and-black butterflies, and begin a fantastic 1,500-mile (2,400-kilometer) migration to wintering grounds in Mexico. It took biologists nearly one hundred years to unravel the life history of these butterflies. Watching them in the milkweed patch made me wonder how much more there is to know about these insects and all the other living organisms in just that one meadow.

The patterns of the natural world have often been likened to a spider's web, and for good reason. All life on Earth is interconnected in an elegant yet surprisingly simple design, and each living thing is an essential part of that design. To understand biology and the functions of living things, biologists have spent a lot of time looking at the differences among organisms. But in order to understand the very nature of living things, we must first understand what they have in common.

The butterfly larvae and the milkweed—and all animals and plants, for that matter—are made up of the same basic elements. These elements are obtained, used, and eliminated by every living thing in a series of chemical activities called metabolism.

Every molecule of every living tissue must contain carbon. During photosynthesis, green plants take in carbon dioxide from the atmosphere. Within their chlorophyll-filled leaves, in the presence of sunlight, the carbon dioxide is combined with water to form sugar—nature's most basic food. Animals need carbon, too. To grow and function, animals must eat plants or other animals that have fed on plants in order to obtain carbon. When plants and animals die, bacteria and fungi help to break down their tissues. This allows the carbon in plants and animals to be recycled. Indeed, the carbon in your body—and everyone else's body—may once have been inside a dinosaur, a giant redwood, or a monarch butterfly!

All life also needs nitrogen. Nitrogen is an essential component of protoplasm, the complex of chemicals that makes up living cells. Animals acquire nitrogen in the same manner as they acquire carbon dioxide: by eating plants or other animals that have eaten plants. Plants, however, must rely on nitrogen-fixing bacteria in the soil to absorb nitrogen from the atmosphere and convert it into proteins. These proteins are then absorbed from the soil by plant roots.

Living things start life as a single cell. The process by which cells grow and reproduce to become a specific organism—whether the organism is an oak tree or a whale—is controlled by two basic substances called deoxyribonucleic acid (DNA) and ribonucleic acid (RNA). These two chemicals are the building blocks of genes that determine how an organism looks, grows, and functions. Each organism has a unique pattern of DNA and RNA in its genes. This pattern determines all the characteristics of a living thing. Each species passes its unique pattern from generation to generation. Over many billions of years, a process involving genetic mutation and natural selection has allowed species to adapt to a constantly changing environment by evolving—changing genetic patterns. The living creatures we know today are the results of these adaptations.

Reproduction and growth are important to every species, since these are the processes by which new members of a species are created. If a species cannot reproduce and adapt, or if it cannot reproduce fast enough to replace those members that die, it will become extinct (no longer exist).

In recent years, biologists have learned a great deal about how living things function. But there is still much to learn about nature. With high-technology equipment and new information, exciting discoveries are being made every day. New insights and theories quickly make many biology textbooks obsolete. One thing, however, will forever remain certain: As living things, we share an amazing number of characteristics with other forms of life. As animals, our survival depends upon the food and functions provided by other animals and plants. As humans—who can understand the similarities and interdependence among living things—we cannot help but feel connected to the natural world, and we cannot forget our responsibility to protect it. It is only through looking at, and understanding, the rest of the natural world that we can truly appreciate what it means to be "alive."

Fungi: The Overview

1

Fungi live almost everywhere on Earth. Bracket fungi form shelf-like growths on tree stumps. White mushrooms grow among grass in backyards. Downy mildew attacks fields of potato plants. Brown rot fungi feed on apples and pears. Rusts injure wheat plants. Mold grows on old bread in kitchens and on damp objects in cellars.

Fungi (singular, fungus) live in fields and forests, hot deserts and icy Arctic lands, deep caves and high mountains, lakes and oceans. Most live in soil and on the dead remains of plants and animals. Others live on living plants and animals, including humans. For example, athlete's foot is caused by a fungus that lives on people's feet.

There is a fascinating variety in the size, shape, and color of fungi. Yeasts are fungi that consist of only a single cell. At the other extreme are puffballs as big as sheep! Some fungi form crust-like growths.

Opposite:
The world of fungi is astonishing in its variety. Fungi range from being microscopic and colorless to being large and brightly colored, as are these fly agaric mushrooms.

Others look like blobs of slimy jelly. Still others are shaped like fingers, cups, or umbrellas. White, black, and every color of the rainbow are represented, from reds and yellows to greens, lavenders, and purples.

Some fungi are able to live in many different habitats, or kinds of places. Others are very fussy. One forest fungus grows only on cones of Douglas fir trees. Wheat rust needs to live on both wheat and barberry plants to complete its life cycle.

Slime Time

Wolf's-milk slime

Slime molds are a particularly strange group of fungi that can change their own shape, color, and texture. Some can transform themselves from gooey, oozing blobs to soft cushion-like masses in just a matter of hours. Slimes differ from other fungi because they begin life as a simple blob of protoplasm (material that makes up cells in all living things). In this stage, slimes have the ability to move and ingest nutrients as they go. Slime molds move themselves with a constant series of expansions and contractions. This process is called protoplasmic streaming.

One of the most interesting things about slimes is the way in which they can take on many weird shapes and textures. Coral slime is an almost see-through mass that produces a series of small structures resembling tiny icicles. Pretzel slime creates intricate overlapping patterns on the surfaces it crosses. Wolf's-milk slime is a reddish mass of rounded "cushions" that ooze a pink paste. And scrambled-egg slime looks incredibly like what its name suggests!

For some reason, many slimes have been named after popular foods—though slime is something you'd never want to eat! In addition to pretzel slime and scrambled-egg slime, there's also carnival candy (cotton candy) slime, red raspberry slime, tapioca slime, and chocolate tube slime!

Pretzel slime

Scrambled-egg slime

Figuring Out Fungi

Fungi are like plants in some ways. They are not, however, true plants. True plants have a green pigment called chlorophyll. Plants use chlorophyll to make food, in a process called photosynthesis. Fungi do not contain chlorophyll, although they may contain other green pigments. Without chlorophyll, fungi cannot make their own food. Instead, they must obtain food from other organisms.

To carry out photosynthesis, plants need light. Fungi do not need light to survive. Many kinds of fungi can live underground and in dark places such as caves and cellars.

Most plants have roots, stems, leaves, and flowers. The body of a fungus does not have these parts. Most plants reproduce by means of seeds, which are complex structures consisting of many cells. Fungi reproduce by means of spores, which usually consist of a single cell.

Fungi are not animals, either. But even though fungi are neither plants nor animals, they share important features with all living organisms. Like plants and animals, they need food, they react to changes in their environment, and they reproduce.

Fungi affect other living things in many ways. Slime molds and bracket fungi help to break down dead organisms. Certain yeasts and blue-green molds are used in making bread, cheese, and medicines. Other fungi are harmful. Black molds destroy human food. Rusts, smuts, and fish molds injure and often kill plants and animals.

The Body of a Fungus

If you were to carefully pull up a mushroom from a backyard or a forest, you would see delicate white threads attached to the mushroom's bottom. These threads are actually the main body of the mushroom. They are called hyphae (singular, hypha). The entire mass of underground hyphae—the mushroom's body—is called a mycelium (plural, mycelia).

A hypha grows at its tip, just like a plant root grows at its tip. Occasionally it branches, and as the branches grow longer, they too branch. The network of hyphae spreads out in all directions. But people do not actually see the hyphae because they are completely underground.

DID YOU KNOW

Thin Thoughts

Some fungi have hyphae that are so thin they can be seen only through a microscope. These hyphae are less than 1/50,000 inch (0.000127 centimeter) in diameter. This means that 50,000 such hyphae would have to be laid side by side to equal a width of one inch (2.5 centimeters).

Anatomy of a Mushroom

When most people think of a mushroom, they think of a fungus that looks like the one shown below—with an umbrella cap and stem. Many mushrooms, however, do not have caps or stalks.

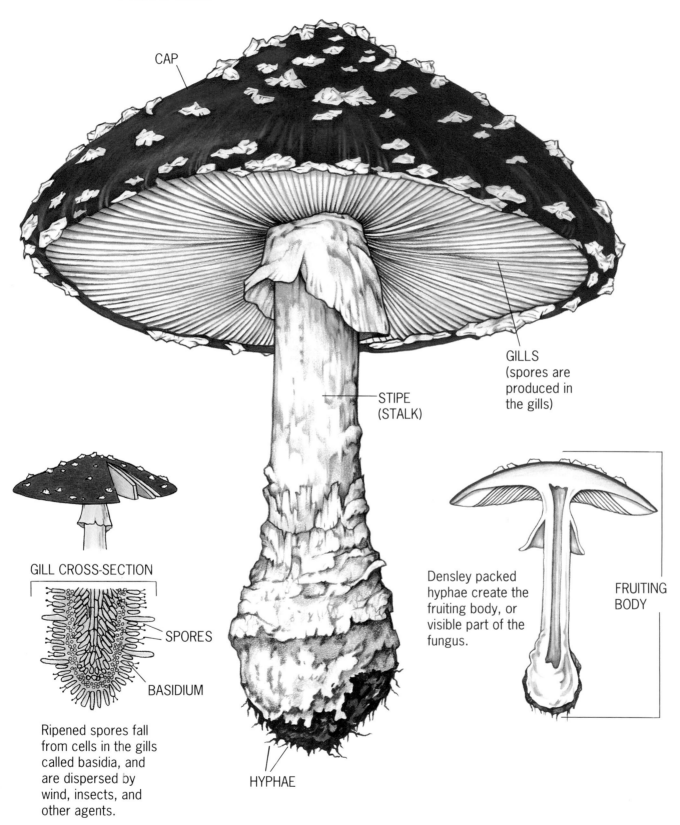

CAP

GILLS
(spores are
produced in
the gills)

STIPE
(STALK)

GILL CROSS-SECTION

SPORES

BASIDIUM

Ripened spores fall
from cells in the gills
called basidia, and
are dispersed by
wind, insects, and
other agents.

HYPHAE

Densley packed
hyphae create the
fruiting body, or
visible part of the
fungus.

FRUITING
BODY

The visible part of the mushroom—the part that grows above the ground—is called the fruiting body. The fruiting body is made up of densely packed hyphae. Its function is to produce spores, which are the reproductive cells of the mushroom. Under the right environmental conditions, the spores germinate, or develop into new mushrooms.

Often, a single mushroom fungus produces many fruiting bodies. Most fruiting bodies have two main parts. The lower, stem-like part is called the stipe, or stalk. The upper part is called the cap. On the underside of many caps are hundreds of thin sheet-like folds called gills. The gills radiate outward from the stipe to the edge of the cap. On the surface of each gill are special cells that bear the spores

Most other fungi also are made up of hyphae. Bread mold consists of white hyphae that grow inside a piece of bread. Sometimes, some of the hyphae grow on the surface of the bread, making the bread look fuzzy. Soon, the bread mold produces fruiting bodies. When the spores in the fruiting bodies mature, they turn black, making the bread look very unappetizing.

Yeasts and slime molds are examples of fungi that do not have mycelia. A yeast organism consists of only a single cell. A slime mold is a jelly-like mass that slowly flows over rotting wood.

DID YOU KNOW

You Should See a Mycologist

The study of fungi is called mycology. This name comes from two Greek words: *mykes*, which means "mushroom," and *logos*, which means "study" or "discuss." Scientists who specialize in the study of fungi are called mycologists.

Below left: The tiny hyphae that make up bread mold give it its fuzzy appearance. *Below middle:* Mushrooms, some of the most common fungi, are made up of densely packed hyphae that form into distinct shapes, such as gills, caps, and stipes. *Below right:* Slime molds are a group of fungi that do not have hyphae or mycelia.

Mushroom Power

The enormous strength of some mushrooms is surprising. When the cells stretch, they act like tiny hydraulic rams that create a slow but steady pressure against any object above the growing mushroom. This steady pressure over a period of time is enough to weaken asphalt and to split concrete. Fruiting mushrooms have been known to push their way up through a 3-inch- (8-centimeter-) thick layer of asphalt, to lift wine casks in a winery high off a cellar floor, and to break through concrete floors in factories. In England, an 83-pound (37-kilogram) stone slab 2 feet (0.7 meter) in diameter was freed of its cement shackles and lifted 2 inches (5 centimeters) off the ground. When British residents actually looked underneath the stone, they found what were probably two small meadow mushrooms balancing the stone in the center!

One of the most dramatic examples of mushroom power was described by Italian mycologists Augusto Rinaldi and Vassili Tyndalo in *The Complete Book of Mushrooms*. Some people in a courtyard heard a loud noise like an exploding firecracker coming from a portico that faced the courtyard. The concrete floor of the portico then split and rose into the air, revealing several compact agaric mushrooms in the floor opening.

The Variety of Fungi

No one is certain how and when the very first fungi developed, or evolved. But we know that fungi have lived on Earth for more than 350 million years. They were here long before humans, horses, flowering plants, and many other familiar kinds of organisms. We know of the ancient fungi from fossils, which are remains or traces of living things that have been preserved in rocks and other materials for thousands or millions of years. Fossilized fungi have been found on sponges and mollusk shells that are hundreds of millions of years old.

Some species of ancient fungi are extinct, that is, they no longer exist. Other ancient species continue to survive. Fossils of diseased ferns that lived 200 million years ago show that the ferns were damaged by a kind of fungus that still exists today.

DID YOU KNOW

Taking the Toad Load

Some people call certain mushrooms "toadstools." Ancient stories say that toads often use these fungi as seats, or stools. It is true that you might see a toad sitting on top of—or next to—a toadstool. But it is not the mushroom that has attracted the toad. The toad is there because many insects feed on mushrooms, and toads think insects are mighty yummy!

The Amazing Variety of Mushrooms

Mushrooms thrive in various environments all over the world. Scientists have identified thousands of mushroom species—more than 3,000 varieties are known to exist in North America alone. Their variety of shapes, colors, and sizes continues to fascinate mycologists and mushroom hunters alike. As you can see from the examples below, many mushrooms do not have the familiar "cap" and "stalk" fruiting bodies that are familiar to most people.

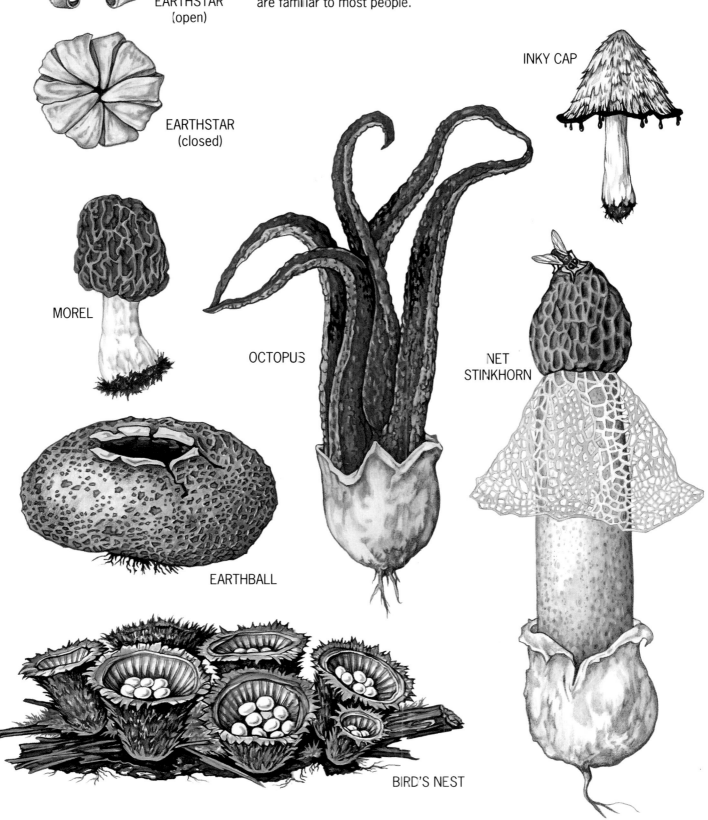

EARTHSTAR
(open)

EARTHSTAR
(closed)

INKY CAP

MOREL

OCTOPUS

NET
STINKHORN

EARTHBALL

BIRD'S NEST

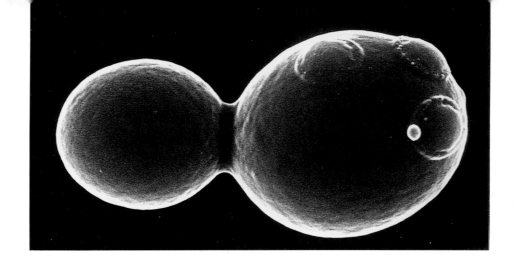

Microscopic yeasts are among the smallest species of fungi. This species of yeast is commonly used in brewing.

Scientists have identified about 100,000 different kinds, or species, of living fungi. The actual number of species is probably much greater. Every year, scientists discover additional species, usually in tropical rainforests and other places that have not been well explored.

Among the smallest species are the one-celled yeasts. They are so small that they can be seen only under a microscope.

Humongous Fungus

When people measure a puffball or a bracket fungus, they are measuring only the fruiting body. If a fungus's mycelium is also included in the measurements, then the total size and weight of the fungus is much, much greater.

In 1992, scientists announced that they had discovered a truly enormous fungus in Michigan. Composed of a network of mushroom fruiting bodies and connecting hyphae, the fungus covered about 38 acres (15 hectares) of forest soil. The scientists estimated that it weighed about 100 tons (91 metric tons). They also estimated that it began growing from a tiny spore at least 1,500 years ago. This made the fungus one of the oldest and largest living things on Earth—and it is still growing!

Giant puffball

The Michigan fungus soon had competition. Scientists reported that a fungus growing in the forests of the state of Washington was 40 times bigger than the Michigan fungus. It covered 1,500 acres (607 hectares)! The scientists suggested that there may be even bigger fungi in other forests of western North America.

The giant Michigan and Washington fungi are closely related. Both are types of armillaria mushrooms.

Fascinating Fungi

Every kind of fungus, like every other kind of living thing, has its own scientific name. This is its species name. But many fungi also have popular names. Some of these names are as colorful as the fungi themselves!

 **Milk Caps** These mushrooms are named for the milky juice, called latex, they produce when broken. There are many species of milk caps. Different species have latex of different colors. For example, one species produces a white latex that quickly changes to bright yellow when exposed to air. Another species produces a white latex that does not change when exposed to air. Still another species, called the bleeding milk cap, produces a dark red latex. Milk caps grow near trees. Some species will grow only near certain kinds of trees. For example, bleeding milk caps grow under Douglas firs in the Pacific Northwest.

 **Witches' Butter** One group of fungi are called jelly fungi because their fruiting bodies look like jelly. Among these species are several called witches' butter. Their yellow fruiting bodies look like oddly shaped chunks of butter. Witches' butter grows on dead branches and logs, and is common in wet weather. It shrivels up in dry weather, but it may expand again when rain returns. Perhaps people once believed that only witches could perform such magic!

 **Orange Peel Fungus** The fruiting bodies of this fungus are easy to identify, because they look very much like pieces of orange peel. They are bright orange, and up to 5 inches (12.5 centimeters) wide. They usually form during moist weather and are most common on hard, bare soil along roads and paths through woodlands. At first, the fruiting body is round. Soon, it opens and looks like a cup or saucer. When several orange peel fungi grow clustered together, the fruiting bodies begin to push against one another, changing their shapes.

 **Fairy Fingers** At the edge of a forest, a cluster of small white "fingers" pokes up through a patch of moss. Each delicate structure is about 4 inches (10 centimeters) high. These are the fruiting bodies of a species of club fungi. The spores are produced on the upper part of each fruiting body. Sometimes people confuse fairy fingers with fungi known as earth tongues. But earth tongues are tougher and the upper part of their fruiting body is flattened or twisted.

 **Chicken-of-the-Woods** Some people think this yellow-orange fungus looks like sulfur ore. Other people say it looks like pieces of candy corn. But most agree that the flesh looks a lot like uncooked chicken meat! Chicken-of-the-woods forms an overlapping cluster of fan-shaped shelves on trees and logs. Each shelf may be 6 inches (15 centimeters) or more across. Like chicken, the young fungus is very tasty if it is cooked properly. Many people hunt for chicken-of-the-woods.

Giant puffballs are usually considered to be among the largest fungi. They sometimes grow to be as big as a sheep or large dog! Usually, however, giant puffballs are about the size of a soccer ball.

Another record holder was a huge bracket fungus found in the state of Washington. It was 56 inches (142 centimeters) long, 37 inches (94 centimeters) wide, and weighed 300 pounds (136 kilograms).

2

The Senses: How Fungi React

Like all living things, fungi must deal with an environment that is constantly changing. Periods of light are followed by periods of darkness. Rainy days, during which the ground becomes soaked with water, are followed by sunny days, when the ground gradually dries. Temperatures change with the seasons, soil chemistry changes from one place to another, smooth surfaces open onto rough surfaces, and each habitat contains its own mix of plants and animals.

Fungi are able to detect changes in the environment that are important to their survival. A change in the environment that can be detected by an organism is called a stimulus (plural, stimuli). The reaction that the organism makes to a stimulus is called a response.

Unlike humans and other animals, fungi do not have special sense organs, such as eyes and ears, that detect stimuli. They do not have a nervous system

Opposite:
Fungi, like all living things, must be able to react to their surroundings in order to survive. Here, a group of honey mushrooms grow out and up in the forest, toward the source of light.

that carries messages from sense organs to other parts of the body. And they do not have muscles that can move the body toward or away from stimuli.

In ways not yet completely understood, fungi seem to receive stimuli through certain cells, such as those at the tips of hyphae. Chemical messages are then sent to other cells, which respond to the stimuli.

Reacting to Light

Some fungi do not seem to be sensitive to light. That is, their growth is not affected by the amount of light or darkness in their environment. But for many other varieties of fungi, light—or the absence of light—is an important stimulus.

Wetter Is Better

An earthstar looks like a little star that has fallen onto the soil of a forest floor. But it is a fungus, and it changes its appearance in response to moisture.

Moisture causes the dark brown outer wall of an earthstar's fruiting body to expand. The wall cracks and splits into star-like rays. These rays curve outward, forming a halo around the pale spore sac. The wall of the spore sac is very thin. When a drop of water falls onto the sac, it pushes in on the wall. This causes spores to shoot out of a hole in the top of the sac.

Some kinds of earthstars will close up during dry weather. The outer pieces curl up and inward to surround and protect the spore sac. This prevents spores from escaping when the earth is dry and their chances of growth are poor. The earthstar may lie curled up for many months until, in response to wet weather, it will open up again.

Spores shoot out of an earthstar after it has been hit by a drop of water.

Light often affects the development and growth of fruiting bodies. For example, the fruiting bodies of many mushrooms grow upward, toward the source of light. If light comes from only one direction, the fruiting body bends in response.

Light also can affect the release of spores from fruiting bodies. In some fungi, spore release is greatly increased by light. In other fungi, spore release is greater in darkness.

Trichoderma is a very tiny fungus in which spore formation is stimulated by light. Scientists have shown this by growing trichoderma in laboratory dishes. A dish that is grown in constant light is soon filled with dark spores. A dish grown in darkness remains pale; hyphae spread through the dish but no spores form. A dish that is exposed to alternating periods of light and darkness develops a pattern of dark rings (spores) and pale rings (no spores).

Reacting to Chemicals

Coming in contact with certain chemicals in the environment can stimulate a variety of responses among fungi. For example, most fungi react badly to large amounts of carbon dioxide. They either stop growing or their hyphae grow away from places with high carbon dioxide concentrations.

Chemicals often trigger the germination of spores. This explains why wheat rust spores begin to develop when they land on wheat plants, but not when they land on maple trees or donkeys. The spores react to specific chemicals given off by the wheat plant.

Similarly, some spores seem to react to certain chemicals produced by the animals that feed on fruiting bodies. The spores of one fungus will germinate only after they have passed through the digestive system of a frog or lizard!

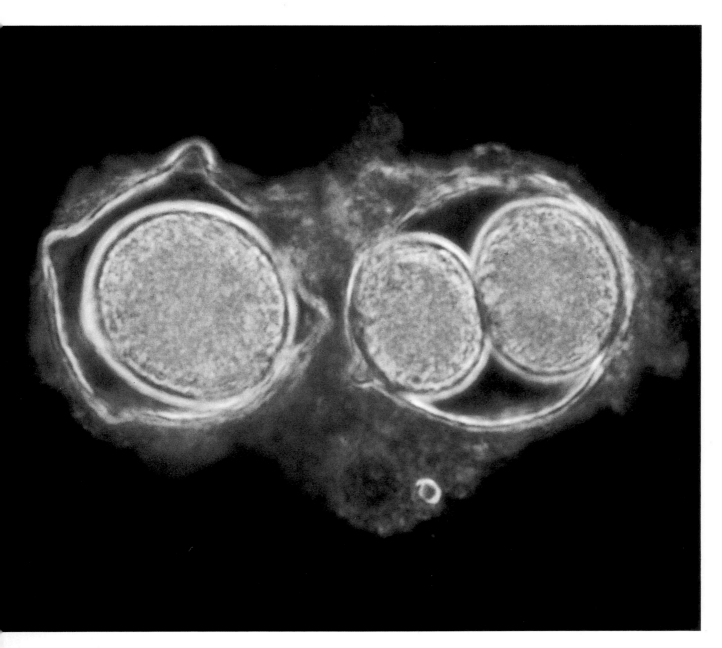

Some fungi, such as certain water molds, release sex hormones into the surrounding water in order to attract other members of the same species.

Chemicals also are involved in reproduction. Some water molds, for example, produce chemicals called sex hormones that they release into the water. The hormones spread through the water and are sensed by the nearby members of the same species. For example, the hyphae of female water molds of certain *Achlya* species give off a certain hormone that causes the hyphae of males to begin producing reproductive structures. These structures then bend toward the female water molds.

Reacting to Other Stimuli

Other environmental stimuli that can affect fungi include gravity, touch, and water.

Gravity Gravity is a force, or pull, exerted by the Earth's mass. The stipe of a common mushroom reacts negatively to gravity. It grows upward, away from the Earth—just as the stem of a tree does. The mushroom's gills react positively to gravity. They grow downward, toward the ground.

Touch Habitats such as tree stumps and small plots of soil are usually home to more than one fungus. What happens when hyphae of two fungi

When the hyphae of two different varieties of fungi meet, they will react by turning away from each other. Here, mushrooms and lichens (which are combinations of fungi and algae) share the surface of a tree stump.

meet? If the hyphae are of two different kinds of fungi, they may react by turning away from one another. But if the hyphae are from two fungi of the same species, they may unite and begin the process of reproduction.

The bean rust fungus, which grows on beans and bean leaves, uses touch to find its way along a leaf. It actually searches for openings in the leaf's surface. These openings are surrounded by ridges of a certain height. There are other ridges on the leaf, but they are either much lower or much higher than those around the openings. The rust fungus ignores these kinds of openings. But when the fungus hyphae feel the ridge around an opening, they begin to form special infection structures.

Bean rust fungus uses a sense of touch to find its way along the plant it is invading.

The Senses: How Fungi React

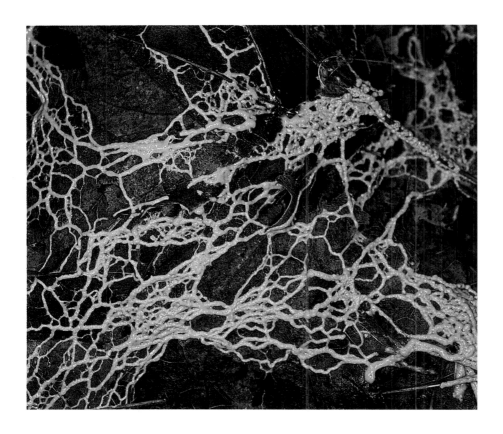

Most fungi react to the presence or the absence of water in their environment. The consistency of slime molds, for example, thickens into a resting stage when little or no water is available.

Water Most fungi prefer damp environments. Hyphae react to dampness by growing more rapidly and by producing fruiting bodies. For example, boletus fungi produce many more mushrooms during a rainy season then during a dry season.

When the amount of moisture in the environment falls, fungal growth slows or even stops. Certain fungi, including some slime molds, change their appearance. In damp weather, a slime mold looks like a slimy mass of jelly. If conditions become too dry, the slime mold may react by changing into a thick resting stage. The length of time it can survive in the resting stage depends on the species. Some slime molds can survive in a resting stage for about a month. Others can survive for up to three years.

Fungal spores react to dampness by germinating. If the spores are in a dry place, they may remain unchanged for many years, waiting for the return of enough moisture before beginning to form hyphae.

3

Metabolism: How Fungi Function

A fungus spore lands on a damp, rotting log in the forest. The spore begins to send out a tiny thread that branches into more hyphae. The hyphae push into the rotting log. They grow deeper and deeper into the log, merging with hyphae from another source. Then, the fungus forms a fruiting structure on the log's surface. Spores develop in the fruiting structure. When the spores are ripe, they are released into the air and carried away by air currents.

Growing, forming fruiting structures, and developing spores—all these activities require energy. A fungus, like other living things, gets the energy it needs from food. Obtaining food, digesting it, and breaking it down for energy involve many chemical reactions. Other life processes, such as reacting to changes in the environment, also involve complex chemical reactions.

Opposite:
Penicillium mold covers a group of tangerines. Molds get the food they need to survive by implanting themselves on host organisms and taking nutrients from them.

The total of all the chemical changes that take place within an organism is called metabolism. It is metabolism that distinguishes living organisms from nonliving things. As long as metabolism functions properly, an organism will remain active and healthy. When metabolism stops, an organism cannot survive and will die.

Getting Food

Like animals, fungi cannot make their own food. They must get their food from outside sources. Slime molds, like animals, eat solid food. They creep over rotting logs or piles of dead leaves—surrounding bacteria, fungus spores, and other particles of food as they move along.

Blue Devils and "Blushrooms"

Some mushrooms change color when they are cut or bruised. This happens because chemicals in the damaged cells are exposed to air. The chemicals react with oxygen in the air, forming new chemicals.

The devil's boletus is a poisonous mushroom that grows under beech, oak, and other trees. It has a large, broad cap. Instead of gills, the underside is dotted with many little pores, through which spores are released. In young mushrooms, the pores are greenish yellow. They turn as red as "devil's blood" when the mushrooms mature. The flesh of the cap is pale olive. But when it is cut, it immediately turns blue.

One species of amanita mushroom that lives under or near live oak trees is known as "the blusher." When its white flesh is exposed to air, it slowly turns red. Insect larvae often dig networks of tunnels into this mushroom to feed on the fungus's flesh. The tunnels are easy to see because the wounded flesh that forms the tunnel walls is red.

A boletus mushroom shows the effects of bruising.

Most fungi, however, cannot take in solid food. The food must be broken down, or digested, before they can absorb it. Fungi do this by releasing digestive chemicals called enzymes. The enzymes ooze out of the hyphae and break down the complex compounds in the food near the hyphae. The complex food compounds are turned into simpler compounds that can be dissolved in water. Then the fungi feed by absorbing the water and the simple compounds contained within it. This takes place through the thin walls of a fungus's hyphae.

Fungi are sometimes divided into two groups, based on their food: saprophytes and parasites. Depending on their age or on certain specific environmental conditions, some fungi may switch from one diet to the other.

A brown rot mold grows on a peach tree. This mold releases enzymes that break down, or digest, the fruit so that its nutrients can be absorbed by the mold.

Metabolism: How Fungi Function

A Saprophyte to Bite

Honey mushrooms

Honey mushrooms are tasty fungi that are usually honey yellow in color. Clusters of the fruiting bodies can often be seen on old tree stumps and fallen branches. The mushrooms live as saprophytes, absorbing the nutrients they need from the dead cells of the stumps and branches.

But honey mushrooms can also become parasites and attack living trees. Under certain environmental conditions, they will produce thick, black structures that look like shoelaces. These structures, called rhizomorphs, grow over long distances through the soil. When a rhizomorph comes in contact with a living tree, it penetrates the tree's roots and forms a network of white hyphae. The hyphae spread through the tree, eventually killing it.

DID YOU KNOW

Glowing and Growing

Looking for wild mushrooms is usually a daytime activity. But you can find jack-o'-lantern mushrooms at night. These unique mushrooms produce a spooky light—just like a Halloween jack-o'-lantern! The light is energy given off by cells in the gills as they respire.

Saprophytes Saprophytic fungi get their food from the dead bodies or waste products of organisms. They live and feed on fallen leaves, pine needles, logs, branches, tree stumps, pine cones, manure, and dead animals. In people's homes, they attack bread, fruit, vegetables, cheese, meat, damp wood, paper, leather, clothing—indeed, anything that was produced from living things.

Most saprophytes feed only on certain foods. One species lives off dead grass. Another thrives on horse manure. Still another feeds on only cast-off hooves of animals. Even closely related species may have different diets. For example, the reddish-brown mycena is a mushroom that grows on old tree stumps and logs, and eats wood. The clean mycena grows on the ground and feeds on dead leaves.

Other fungi are like people—they eat lots of different foods. Shaggy mane mushrooms feed on a variety

28

Shaggy mane mushrooms are saprophytes that feed on a wide variety of foods. Because of their adaptable diets, they are able to survive in many different kinds of environments.

Metabolism: How Fungi Function

of buried plant matter. Because they have a varied diet, they can live in many different habitats. Shaggy manes are common on lawns and tennis courts, along roads and railroad tracks, and around abandoned buildings. Their bell-shaped caps, decorated with shaggy, upturned scales, make them easy to identify.

Parasites Parasitic fungi can obtain their food directly from the bodies of other living organisms. They invade—and sometimes kill—the creatures on which they live, which are called hosts.

Like saprophytes, parasites may be very choosy about what they feed on. Many species will grow on only one host or on a group of closely related host species. Corn smut grows on corn plants, on or about the ears. It causes big, ugly tumors that make the ears worthless to farmers. Witches'-broom-of-cherry forms broom-like fruiting structures on various kinds of cherry trees, as well as on several kinds of plums. It eventually damages the tree branches so that they cannot bear fruit.

Using Food

Another essential part of metabolism involves taking in oxygen. Oxygen is needed for respiration. During respiration, oxygen combines with food and breaks it down. As the food is broken down into simpler substances, energy is released. This energy is then used by the cells of the organism's body to carry out their activities.

Most fungi get oxygen from the air around them. Even species that lie underground come in contact with tiny pockets of air. Species that live in water get oxygen from the water.

Fungi absorb the oxygen they need through the walls of their hyphae. During respiration and other activities, wastes are produced. These have to be

Corn smut is a parasitic fungus that only grows on corn. It takes the food it needs from the corn, which harms the plant and makes it inedible for humans.

removed, or excreted, from the organisms. Wastes pass out of the fungi through the walls of the hyphae. Slime molds do not have hyphae, but they also absorb oxygen and excrete wastes through the walls of their bodies. Also, slime molds sometimes leave waste particles behind as they move along—just like some people drop litter on a sidewalk as they walk along!

Metabolism: How Fungi Function

Reproduction and Growth

4

An amanita mushroom produces more amanitas. A shaggy mane mushroom produces more shaggy manes. A jelly fungus produces more jelly fungi. This process of forming new organisms of the same kind is called reproduction. Because it is needed for the survival of the species, reproduction is extremely important. If members of a species do not reproduce, the species eventually dies out, or becomes extinct.

Fungi reproduce by forming spores. These are extremely small, usually one-celled structures. They are much simpler than the seeds of trees or the fertilized eggs of mammals. But like seeds and eggs, each spore contains all the information needed to develop into a new organism.

Most fungi produce spores in one of two different ways—asexually and sexually. Asexual reproduction involves only one parent. The fungi that grow from

Opposite:
A thriving colony of collybia mushrooms grows on a moss-covered rock. Reproduction is one of the most important functions carried out by any living organism because new members of a species are constantly needed to replace those that die.

DID YOU KNOW

That Mold Black Magic...

Does your home contain black mold spores? Here is an easy way to answer this question: Moisten a piece of bread and place it on a dish. Expose the bread to the air for a day, then cover it, making certain that it is still moist. Place the covered dish in a warm, dark spot. Observe the bread every day.

If spores fall on the bread, they will soon begin to grow. In several days, you should see signs that a new generation of spores is being produced.

A microphotograph shows spores from the rose leaf rust fungus. Spores, which are the structures that fungi use to reproduce, contain all the information needed to produce new organisms.

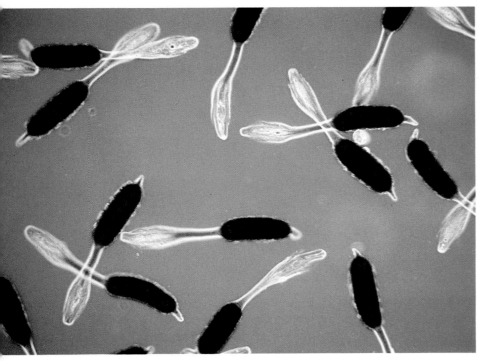

these spores are exactly like the parent, because they got all their genetic (hereditary) material from that parent. Sexual reproduction involves two parents. In this process, the spores contain genetic material from both parents. They develop into fungi that resemble both parents, but are not exactly like either parent.

Many Kinds of Spores

Spores come in many different shapes, sizes, and colors. These characteristics are very useful in identifying spores and the species that produced them. Some fungal species produce round or egg-shaped spores; others produce spores shaped like miniature kidney beans, bananas, or macaroni. Some spores have thick walls; others have thin walls. Some are smooth; others are covered with spines, ridges, or bumps. Some are white or black; others are yellow, pink, green, or brown.

Many fungi that live in water produce spores that are adapted for floating or moving in water. For example, water molds, which live in fresh water and in wet soil, produce spores that have special tail-like appendages that are called flagella. The spores can swim by wiggling their flagella back and forth.

Too small to see Can you see fungi spores in the air around you? No. Are there fungi spores in the air around you? Probably. But you do not see them because the spores are extremely tiny.

Scientists measure the size of spores in units called microns. There are about 25,000 microns in 1 inch (2.5 centimeters). Most fungi produce spores that are 5 to 10 microns long. Some produce spores that are as big as 30 microns. Even these "big" spores can be seen only with the aid of a microscope.

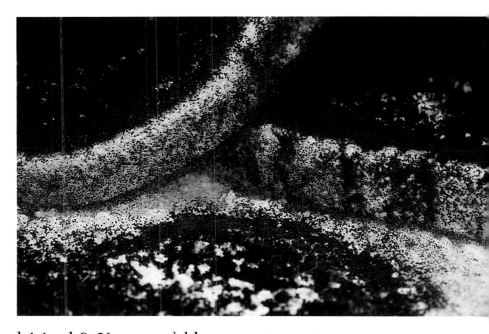

The black, fuzzy appearance of bread mold is created by millions of tiny, ripe spores that can be seen when the sporangia burst open.

How many spores equal 1 inch? You would have to lay 800 30-micron-long spores end to end to equal 1 inch. Or you could lay 4,800 5-micron-long spores end to end to equal 1 inch.

How Fungi Produce Spores

Fruiting bodies and spores are formed in various ways by different fungi. Let's look at several common fungi and how they reproduce.

Bread mold The most common fungus found in homes is probably the black mold that grows on bread. If a moist piece of bread is left on a table for several days, spores in the air settle on the bread and begin to grow. A thick white mycelium develops. Most of the hyphae that make up the mycelium are within the bread, but some hyphae extend sideways along the surface of the bread. And some hyphae are upright. A ball-like capsule, called a sporangium, forms at the tip of each upright hypha. Spores develop within the sporangium. When the spores are ripe, the outer wall of the sporangium splits open and the tiny spores drift away. Those that fall in suitable habits will grow into new molds

The delicate gills underneath the cap of a mushroom contain cells that produce spores. The spores are housed in the gills until air currents or insects carry them to a new location.

Field mushrooms The mycelium of a common field mushroom fungus is a tangled mass of underground hyphae. When temperature and moisture conditions are favorable and the hyphae have absorbed enough food, the mycelium begins to swell at certain points. Each swelling quickly grows into a fruiting body that pushes its way upward, toward the surface.

At first, a fruiting body is shaped like a button. As it grows longer, it takes on the familiar umbrella shape of a cap and stalk. The function of the cap is to produce spores. The function of the stalk is to hold the cap up, away from the ground, so that the spores can be easily scattered.

As the fruiting body pushes its way through the soil, the cap is kept closed by a protective veil. Once the fruiting body is above ground, the veil breaks and the cap opens. The gills on the underside of the newly opened cap are pink. Along their sides are special cells that produce the spores. As the spores develop and ripen, they turn purple or dark brown and completely cover the gills. When the spores are mature, they fall down between the gills. Air currents then carry them off to new homes.

Yeasts To reproduce sexually, two yeast cells join together to form one cell. As this cell grows larger, four or eight spores form within it. When the spores are mature, they break out of the cell and develop into new yeast cells.

More often, yeasts reproduce asexually by a process called budding. A small projection, or bud, forms

The Fi-Nest Fungi

The fruiting bodies of some species of fungi look like little bird's nests. They are no bigger than pennies, yet each contains several tiny "eggs." Each egg-shaped body is filled with spores. During a rainstorm, raindrops bounce the spore containers out of their nest. Eventually, the "eggshells" break and the spores are released into the air.

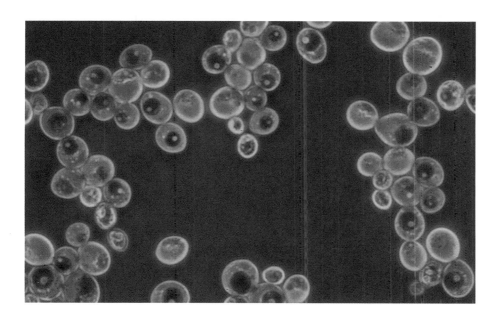

Yeasts most often reproduce asexually through a process called budding. Here, budding yeast cells remain attached to their parents, forming small colonies.

on the side of the parent cell. The bud grows until it reaches a certain size. Then it may separate from the parent cell. Or it may remain attached to the parent as it produces a bud of its own. In this case, the connected yeast cells soon form a small, branched colony.

Wheat rust This is among the most destructive of all organisms. Each year, wheat rust ruins millions of dollars worth of wheat crops. To complete its life cycle, this fungal parasite must alternate between two different kinds of hosts.

In late spring, rust-colored spores are formed on infected wheat plants. Air currents carry these spores to nearby wheat plants. In 10 days, more rust-colored spores, which will infect still other wheat plants, begin to be produced on the newly infected plants. This process continues throughout the summer.

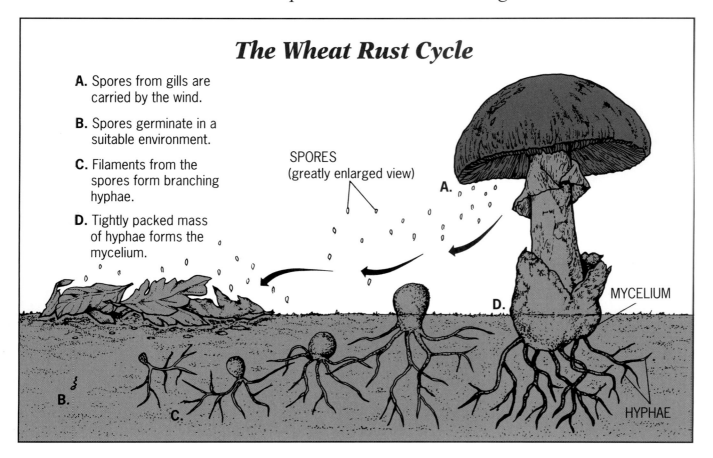

The Wheat Rust Cycle

A. Spores from gills are carried by the wind.

B. Spores germinate in a suitable environment.

C. Filaments from the spores form branching hyphae.

D. Tightly packed mass of hyphae forms the mycelium.

SPORES
(greatly enlarged view)

A.

D.

MYCELIUM

HYPHAE

B.

C.

Individual mushroom spores are too small to be seen without a microscope or magnifying glass. Because each mushroom produces many millions of spores, however, you can see their color by making what are called spore prints.

Take a mushroom whose cap has opened so that the gills can be seen. Gently pull off the stem, taking care not to damage the cap. Lay the cap, gill side down, on a piece of white paper. Cover the cap with a jar or glass to prevent air from blowing away the spores.

Several hours later, carefully lift up the glass and the mushroom cap. The paper will be covered by a pattern of spores that matches the arrangement of the mushroom's gills. No two species of mushrooms produce exactly the same spore print. You can prove this to yourself by making spore prints of different kinds of mushrooms.

(Hint: If the mushroom's spores are white, they will be invisible on white paper. You will have to use black paper for your spore print.)

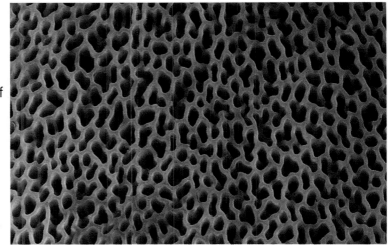

Enlarged view of the spore-bearing surface of a mushroom.

In early fall, the wheat rust fungus produces a different kind of spore. These are black, with thick walls. They do not infect other plants. Rather, their purpose is to enable the species to survive the cold temperatures of winter.

In spring, when temperatures rise, the black spores undergo a series of changes. Each produces four new spores, which are released into the air. To survive, these spores must land on the leaves of a barberry plant. Those that are successful germinate and send hyphae into the leaf tissues. Soon, the hyphae produce reproductive structures, which produce still another kind of spore. These spores cannot infect barberry plants, but they can infect wheat plants. When the spores land on wheat plants and begin to germinate, the life cycle is complete.

DID YOU KNOW

More Spore Lore

Both fungus spores and plant seeds grow into new organisms if conditions are favorable. But spores and seeds are very different in structure. A fungal spore usually consists of only one cell. A plant seed consists of many cells.

A spore contains little or no food; the young fungus must quickly begin to absorb food from its surroundings. Many seeds contain large amounts of food. This built-in food supply nourishes the new plant until it grows leaves and is able to make its own food.

How Fungi Scatter Their Spores

Most fungi produce enormous numbers of spores. A single kernel of wheat infected with wheat smut may contain 12 million smut spores. A field mushroom may produce 2 billion spores.

It would not help the wheat smut or mushroom if all those spores fell near the parent. When the spores began to grow, they would compete with the parent for space, food, water, and air. Few, if any, of the young fungi could survive. But if the spores are scattered over a wide area, more may find conditions suitable for their survival.

Fungi have developed many methods of scattering spores. In general, these methods are similar to those used by green plants to scatter seeds. Wind, rain, water currents, insects, and birds spread spores far and wide. People are important agents of spore dispersal, too. They accidentally carry fungus spores with them as they travel—on foods, crop plants, clothing, lumber, furniture, and other objects—even on their own bodies!

Soon after the fruiting bodies discharge their spores, they die and decay. But the mycelium that produced the fruiting bodies usually continues to live. Eventually, the mycelium will produce more fruiting bodies.

Stinkhorns Many fungi that depend on animals to spread their spores have developed interesting ways to stimulate the senses of animals they wish to attract. Among the masters of this behavior are the stinkhorns. They produce an odor that smells like rotting animal flesh. To humans, the odor stinks. But to flies, it smells like a sweet perfume.

Stinkhorns usually grow in forests. Even if they are buried beneath dead leaves on the forest floor, they can be found by their strong odor.

Stinkhorns produce a strong odor that attracts insects. When the insects land on the fungus, they pick up spores that are then carried to other areas when the insects fly away.

The fruiting body of a common stinkhorn has a white stalk that is topped with a cone-shaped cap. The cap is covered with a strong-smelling slime that contains thousands of spores. The slime attracts flies that like to feed on rotting meat. As the flies crawl over the tip of the stinkhorn, spores stick to their bodies. When the flies leave, they carry away the spores. Eventually, the spores fall off. If the spores land in a suitable place, they will begin to grow.

Black truffles, which grow entirely underground, are a highly prized—and extremely expensive—delicacy around the world.

Truffles Truffles are a type of fungus that grows entirely underground. Even the round, lumpy fruiting bodies form underground. When the spores are ripe, the fruiting bodies give off a strong odor. Animals such as mice, squirrels, and bears smell this odor and start digging. They eat the tasty fruiting bodies, including the spores. But the animals cannot digest the spores. Eventually, the spores are excreted in the animals' droppings. If the spores are dropped in a suitable habitat, they will begin to grow.

People also think truffles are tasty. Truffle hunters in France train dogs and pigs to sniff out truffles. The animals are kept on long leashes as they hunt. When an animal smells a truffle and starts digging it out of the ground, its owner pulls it away and gives it something else to eat. For example, a pig may be given an acorn. While the pig eats the acorn, the person digs up the truffle.

This Is Spore-Ring

One day, a lawn or pasture is a sea of green grass. The next day, as if by magic, a ring of white mushrooms decorates the grassy field. Long ago, people believed that the rings were made by dancing fairies. That's why these mushroom groupings were called fairy rings. Today, we know that each fairy ring develops from a single spore and that all the mushrooms in the ring are part of the same organism.

When the spore of a fairy-ring mushroom germinates, hyphae begin to grow outward in all directions. If nothing is in the way, the mycelium forms an almost perfect underground circle. About once a year, when weather conditions are right, fruiting bodies pop up at the outer edge of the mycelium. They form the fairy ring.

Fairy-ring mushrooms

The mushrooms soon wither and die, but the mycelium continues to spread outward in the soil. Each year, a new fairy ring appears. It is bigger than the fairy ring formed the previous year, when the mycelium was smaller.

Scientists have studied how far the mycelium grows each year. Using this information, they have discovered that some fairy rings are hundreds of years old—and still growing bigger! In Kansas, fairy rings more than 600 feet (183 meters) in diameter began growing about the same time that Columbus landed in the New World.

Fake Flower Fungus

In spring, the meadows of Colorado are filled with flowers. Among these organisms are certain bright yellow flowers that are very popular with insects. There is only one problem: The flowers are fake. They are made by a kind of rust fungus called puccinia. The purpose of puccinia's masquerade is to use insects to help carry out its sexual reproduction.

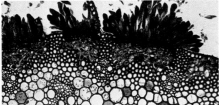

Puccinia infects rock cress plants and causes them to change their shape. Some of the rock cress leaves are twisted into a flower-like structure, then topped with hundreds of small fungal cups filled with sex cells. The fungus even produces a sweet-smelling nectar similar to that produced by real flowers.

Microphotograph of puccinia.

Flies and other insects are attracted by the nectar. As the insects crawl over the fungal cups and lap up the nectar, some of the sex cells stick to their bodies. Later, when the insects visit another fake flower, the sex cells fall off. They join with the sex cells of the second "flower" to form spores.

When the spores are ripe, they are discharged into the air. Those that land on rock cress will eventually germinate and produce more fake flowers.

Germination and Growth

Imagine if every fungus spore developed into a new organism. The world would be buried in fungi! Fortunately, very few spores ever land in places that provide the right conditions for growth. The great majority of spores never germinate.

When environmental conditions are favorable, spores may begin to germinate soon after they have been released from the parent fungus. But if temperature, moisture, and other conditions are not favorable, the spores remain dormant. Some spores can survive for 20 years or more and still be able to germinate.

As germination begins, a spore starts to swell. It sends out a tiny tube, that branches into hyphae. The hyphae absorb food from their surroundings, and they get longer and longer. As they branch, they may even join with hyphae produced by other spores of the same species, forming a tangled mat of mycelia.

Some fungi may also produce thick, rope-like rhizomorphs. Each rhizomorph actually is a bundle of tightly packed hyphae.

5

Fitting into the Web of Life

Imagine what our planet would be like if nothing ever decayed: if every dead tree and dandelion, every dead fish and dinosaur, every dead bird and human lay unchanged forever and ever. Soon the Earth would be buried beneath great masses of dead organisms. There would not be any room for new organisms. Even if plant seeds did manage to find a bare patch of ground in which to sprout, the soil would not contain the nutrients they need for growth.

Thanks mainly to saprophytic fungi and bacteria, this nightmare does not come true.

At the End of Food Chains

A food chain describes who eats what. All food chains begin with a producer, which is an organism that makes food by the process of photosynthesis. Green plants and algae are producers. All animals are

Opposite:
Leafcutter ants work to create their own colonies of fungi for food. As both decomposers and food sources, fungi play many essential roles in the natural world.

consumers. Some consumers eat producers. Others eat the animals that ate the producers. Of course, many producers and consumers do not get eaten, but they eventually die. Then decomposers, the third basic type of organism found in nature, do their job.

Decomposers break down dead organisms. They do this by digesting the organisms—much as your body breaks down food you eat through the process of digestion. The main decomposers are saprophytic fungi and bacteria. These organisms also break down waste materials produced by living things. They break down fallen leaves, branches, and flowers; animal manure, skins shed by snakes; and so on.

The end products of decomposition are carbon dioxide, nitrates, and other simple chemicals. The decomposers actually use some of these chemicals to grow. But most of the chemicals end up in the air, water, and soil. They become available to green plants and algae, which need to absorb these chemicals so they can make food and grow.

If decomposers do not constantly release these important chemicals into the environment, green plants and algae would be unable to make their own food. The plants and algae would die and the animals

Fungi Feasts

A large cow grazing in a field comes upon a cluster of mushrooms. Chomp! The mushrooms disappear into the cow's mouth. Cows are not the only animals that make fungi a part of their diet. Squirrels, rabbits, mice, deer, and pigs eat them. Even meat-eating animals such as wolves occasionally eat them. And so do humans.

Some insects also eat fungi. Many beetles and flies lay their eggs in bracket fungi. When the young insects hatch, they are surrounded by food!

All these fungi-feeders only eat the fruiting bodies. Because they do not eat the mycelia, they do not kill the fungi. The mycelia continue to grow and eventually produce new fruiting bodies.

Fitting into the Web of Life

Orange fuzz-cone slime covers the surface of a dead tree in the forest. Slime molds are some of the most efficient decomposers in nature.

that fed on those organisms would starve to death. Then the animals that ate the plant-eaters would also starve to death. Soon, the Earth would no longer be home to living things.

Partners in Life

Some kinds of fungi form very special relationships with organisms of other species. Both partners in such a relationship benefit. They help one another survive, often in places where neither could live alone. Here are three examples:

Living with trees Many trees live in close association with certain mushrooms. The fungi hyphae cover and sometimes penetrate tree roots as they extend out into the soil. They also absorb water and minerals from the soil, which they pass on to the tree. In exchange, they absorb food from the tree. These fungi are especially helpful to trees that live in poor-quality soil, such as sandy soil near seashores.

Living with algae Lichens are associations of fungi and algae. A tiny green or blue-green alga lives among the fungi hyphae. The fungus protects the alga against drying out. It also obtains water and minerals needed by itself and the alga. The alga manufactures food for itself and its partner.

Lichens can usually be seen on tree bark, rocks, and stone walls. They also grow on wooden objects such as fence posts and roof shingles. There are three main forms. Crustose lichens form hard, flat crusts. Foliose lichens look like tiny flat leaves. Fruticose lichens look either like little shrubs or long, branched tassels that hang from tree branches. In every case, the shape is unique; it could not be produced by either the fungus or the algae living alone.

Living with ants Texas leaf-cutting ants cultivate fungus gardens. The ants cut pieces off plant leaves and carry the pieces to special chambers in their nest. Living in these chambers are fungi that feed on the leaves. The ants then feed on the fungi. When some of the ants leave the colony to form new colonies, they carry along some of the fungus spores, so they can start their own gardens in their new nests.

Sizing Up Mushrooms

In recent years, there has been a big drop in the number of mushrooms growing in European forests. There has also been a big drop in the average size of mushrooms. Many more mushrooms are needed to equal 1 pound (0.5 kilogram) than were needed several decades ago.

No one is certain what has caused these changes, but the number-one suspect is air pollution from factories, farms, and automobiles. As the amount of sulphur oxides, nitrogen oxides, and other air pollutants increases, the growth of fungi seems to decrease.

Scientists are worried that the decline in fungi will harm Europe's forests. Many trees in the forests depend on fungi growing in close association with their roots. Without these fungi, the trees are not as healthy. They may age and die more quickly.

Is the same problem occurring in North America? No one knows. Europeans have kept records of mushroom populations for many decades. Americans have not kept records for such long periods, so they do not know if the North American continent is also losing these valuable organisms.

Lichens come in three basic forms. Crustose lichens (*top left*) form hard, flat crusts.
Foliose lichens (*right*) are densely packed bunches of small, flat leaves. Fruticose lichens
(*bottom left*) develop into bunches of twisted, branching structures.

Consumers and Bloomers

Parasites are a kind of consumer, since they feed on other organisms. Many fungi are parasites on plants and animals, but some are parasites on other fungi.

Some milk mushrooms have white caps. Sometimes, the caps of these mushrooms are covered with an orange coat made up of parasitic fungi. The parasites feed on, and eventually kill, the milk mushrooms.

Another parasitic fungus attacks amanita mushrooms, including the very poisonous amanita known as the "Destroying Angel" or the "Angel of Death." When an amanita is attacked by the parasite, its shape becomes so deformed that it no longer looks like a mushroom.

Fungi and Humans

Fungi are important to people in many ways; they can be both harmful and helpful.

Fungi as pests Fungi cause thousands of diseases, many of which harm humans, their crops, and the animals they raise. Plants in particular suffer great damage from fungi. Wheat may be the victim of more than 300 different species of rust fungi. Rusts also infect other food crops, including oats, corn, rye, beets, peas, pears, and cherries. Rusts kill valuable trees, too, including hemlocks, pines, coffee trees, and fig trees.

Smuts—named for the black mass of spores they produce—attack the flowers of grasses and cereals. Wheat and corn smuts destroy millions of dollars worth of crops each year.

Powdery mildews usually grow as parasites on the leaves of flowering plants. Their spores give the

Famine by Fungus

Humans have often carried organisms from one environment to another. They may do this on purpose, or they may do it accidentally. Introducing an organism into a new environment can have terrible consequences.

Potatoes are native to South America. Europeans first learned of potatoes when Spanish explorers carried some home from South America in the sixteenth century. During the next 200 years, potatoes became an important crop throughout Europe, but especially in Ireland.

Another organism that originated in South America is a fungus that causes a disease called potato blight. This fungus was also carried to Europe, though not on purpose. During the 1840s, potato blight arrived in Ireland. Before people could try to control its spread, it totally destroyed Ireland's potato crop for two years in a row. A great famine and mass starvation resulted. About 1 million people died and more than 1 million other people left Ireland and emigrated to North America in search of better lives.

Scientists have developed ways to control potato blight, but the fungus still causes lots of trouble. Farmers must constantly guard against it.

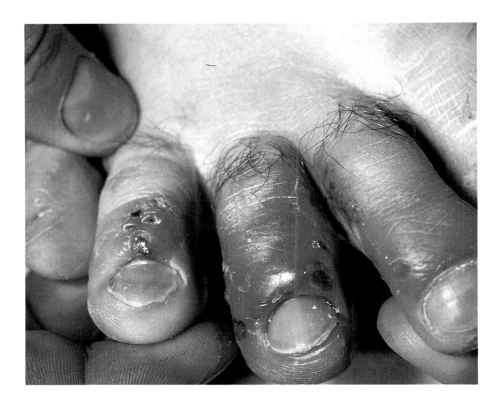

Athlete's foot is caused by a common variety of ringworm, which is really not a worm but rather a kind of fungus. As the fungus grows, it forms ring-like markings on the skin it infects.

infected parts a white, powdery appearance. Apple trees, grapevines, and rose and lilac bushes often suffer powdery mildew infections.

Some fungi live on animal skin, fur, and feathers. They seldom kill the animals, but they do cause pain. One group of fungi that infects humans are the dermatophytoses. They cause diseases called ringworm—the name comes from the round, ring-shaped wounds often made by the fungi. Dermatophytoses can infect almost any part of a person's skin, hair, or nails. One of the most common forms of ringworm is athlete's foot.

Fungi that grow in people's homes are also a real nuisance, particularly in damp climates. Molds spoil fruit, bread, and other food. Mildews destroy clothing, books, and other objects. Spores of various kinds cause allergic reactions in many people.

Over time, people have developed ways to control the damage caused by parasitic fungi. One method is to use chemicals called fungicides to kill fungi or to

DEADLY GALERINA

SWEATING MUSHROOM

BIG LAUGHING MUSHROOM

Killer Mushrooms

Mushrooms that are sold in stores are mostly grown on farms and are safe to eat. Many mushrooms that grow in the wild are also safe to eat. But some wild mushrooms can cause serious illness and even death if they are eaten. The mushrooms shown here range from the mildly poisonous to the deadliest.

Most deaths from mushroom poisoning are caused by certain kinds of amanita mushrooms. One common species, found in North America and Europe, is a slender, graceful beauty. But one nibble of its white flesh is enough to kill an adult human. Scientists named this amanita species *Amanita virosa*. Other people commonly refer to it as the "Angel of Death" or the "Destroying Angel."

There are no simple tests that can determine whether or not a mushroom is edible or poisonous. Some people wrongly think that poisonous mushrooms are most often brightly colored, but this is not true.

GREEEN GILL

POISONOUS BOLETUS

FLY AGARIC

DESTROYING ANGEL

PANTHER AMANITA

The only way to know for sure is to be certain of the species and to have enough experience in identifying various types of mushrooms. Although relatively few mushrooms cause life-threatening illnesses, many can cause serious poisoning, hallucinations, and other severe reactions. Some common symptoms of mushroom poisoning include nausea, vomiting, and diarrhea. In the most serious cases, liver or kidney failure can occur, followed by death. If a person suspects that poisoning has occurred, medical attention is needed immediately. If at all possible, an uncooked sample of the suspected mushroom should be brought to the doctor for inspection.

Hunting mushrooms can be fun, but touching and tasting them can be very dangerous. Many poisonous mushrooms look harmless to the average person. And many poisonous species look surprisingly similar to edible species. Only real experts can tell the difference. For this reason, people should never taste wild mushrooms unless an expert first makes sure that they are suitable for human consumption.

FALSE MOREL

INKY CAP

Many kinds of mushrooms are popular foods for humans. Millions of tons of common mushrooms—along with oyster mushrooms, shiitake mushrooms, and straw mushrooms—are grown each year on commercial farms around the world.

There's a Fungus Amongus

During the American Revolution, fungi acted as secret agents for the American colonies, which were fighting for independence from Britain. The British Navy had the finest warships in the world. But like all ships of that time, they were built of wood. The damp wood was an attractive environment for fungi. As the fungi grew, they rotted the wood and destroyed the ships. More British ships actually sank during the war from the effects of fungi than from the efforts of the colonists!

prevent them from reproducing. Another method is to remove and destroy infected organisms, such as infected trees. This helps to prevent the spread of disease to healthy organisms. Still another method is to create organisms that are resistant to fungi. This has been very effective with certain crop plants. For example, scientists have created varieties of wheat that are resistant to rust fungi.

Fungi as helpers Fungi's role in the process of decay is certainly one of their most important contributions to humans, as well as to all other living things. But humans have also found other uses for fungi.

Some fungi, especially certain mushrooms, are valuable sources of food. In addition to being tasty, the fungi provide essential minerals and vitamins.

Each year, millions of tons of mushrooms are grown commercially all over the world. People also gather and eat wild mushrooms, a practice that requires an excellent knowledge of species, since some mushrooms are poisonous.

Yeasts are important because of their unusual method of respiration. When yeasts are put in an environment where they cannot get oxygen, they change sugar into carbon dioxide and alcohol. This is called fermentation. Yeasts are used in the production of beer, wine, and liquors.

One kind of yeast, called baker's yeast, is used to make bread light and fluffy. The yeast breaks down sugar in the bread dough, producing carbon dioxide gas and alcohol. Bubbles of carbon dioxide cause the dough to expand, or rise. The heat of baking causes the bubbles in the dough to expand still more. Meanwhile, the alcohol is given off into the air.

Certain blue and green molds are used in making foods. The bluish veins and distinctive flavor of Roquefort cheese are due to the presence of a species of penicillium mold. The characteristic flavor of Camembert cheese is created by spreading another species of penicillium mold over the ripening cheese. And the lemony flavor of many candies and soft drinks comes from citric acid produced not by any lemons but by an aspergillus mold.

A small species of penicillium mold is the source of the medicine called penicillin. Penicillin was discovered in 1928 by the Scottish scientist Alexander Fleming. Fleming was growing colonies of bacteria on dishes in his laboratory. One day, he noticed that mold had grown in some of the dishes. Instead of just throwing out the dishes, he took a closer look. As he inspected the containers, he saw that no bacteria were growing near the mold. Fleming investigated

Fitting into the Web of Life

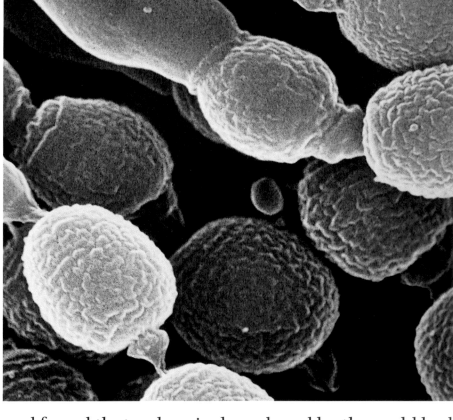

A microphotograph of the penicillium mold used to create penicillin. Various species of molds are also commonly used in the production of cheeses, candies, and other food products.

DID YOU KNOW

Poison Producers

Many organisms produce poisons to protect themselves against attack. Some trees produce chemicals that prevent fungi from growing on them. Some fungi produce poisons to prevent other fungi and bacteria from growing near them. Substances produced by living things that kill or slow the growth of other living things are called antibiotics. This name comes from two Greek words meaning "against life." People have learned how to use some antibiotics to kill disease-causing organisms.

and found that a chemical produced by the mold had killed the bacteria. He named this chemical penicillin and suggested that it might be valuable in treating certain human illness.

Following Fleming's discovery, scientists developed other medicines from fungi. For example, streptomycin and terramycin are bacteria-killers made from species of streptomyces fungi. Medicines made from fungi are very valuable in the fight against disease. They have saved the lives of millions of people. They have also been very helpful in protecting farm animals and crops against deadly diseases that could destroy food supplies.

The more we learn about fungi, the more we appreciate their importance to humans and other living things. Like all organisms, fungi are an essential part of the precious environment that we all share on Earth.

Classification Chart of Fungi

Kingdom: Fungi

About 100,000 different species of fungi have been identified by scientists. These species can be classified in seven phylum. (Different scientists use different classification systems.)

Phylum	Typical Members	Characteristics
Myxomycota (Slime mold)	wolf's-milk fungi, fuligo (flowers of tan), stemonitis ceratiomyxa	constantly change their shape; when a spore germinates, it produces a cell that has one or two whip-like flagella
Oomycota (Egg-like fungi)	water molds, downy mildews	consist of either a single cell or a mass of hyphal threads; hyphae are branches of hollow tubes
Basidiomycota (Club fungi)	rusts and smuts, coral fungi, bracket fungi, pore fungi, mushrooms, puffballs, stinkhorns	produce spores externally on club-shaped structures called basidia
Ascomycota (Sac fungi)	yeasts blue and green molds, powdery mildews, cup fungi (truffles, morels), sphere fungi	produce spores in closed sacs called asci
Deuteromycota (Imperfect fungi)	fungi that cause athlete's foot and other ringworm, leaf spot, fruit rot, clothing mold; penicillium, aspergillus	reproduction appears to be by asexual spores only (the life cycle of many is unknown or incompletely known)
Mycophycota (Fungus algae)	lichens	associations of certain fungi and algae, in which both species benefit
Zygomycota (Yolk fungi)	black molds, dung fungi	produce spores in structures formed on branches of the mycelium

Dinoflagellata DINOFLAGELLATES	*Chrysophyta* YELLOW-GREEN, GOLDEN ALGAE
Protozoa PROTOZOANS	*Bacillariophyta* DIATOMS
Phaeophyta BROWN ALGAE	*Rhodophyta* RED ALGAE

Euglenophyta EUGLENOID FLAGELLATES	*Cryptophyta* CRYPTOMONADS
Gamophyta CONJUGATING GREEN ALGAE	*Chlorophyta* GREEN ALGAE
Myxomycota SLIME MOLDS	*Oomycota* DOWNY MILDEWS, POTATO BLIGHT
Basidiomycota SMUTS, RUSTS, JELLY FUNGI, MUSHROOMS, PUFFBALLS, STINKHORNS	*Deuteromycota* PENICILLIUM, ASPERGILLUS, CANDIDA
Mycophycota LICHENS	*Zygomycota* BLACK MOLDS, DUNG FUNGI
	Ascomycota YEASTS, MORELS, TRUFFLES

Biological Classification

For a long time, plants were considered one of two kingdoms that classified all living things on Earth. The two kingdoms were the plant kingdom and the animal kingdom. As scientists studied the approximately 400,000 different kinds of plants, however, they began to realize that many did not fit well into either the plant or the animal kingdom. In response to this problem, scientists began to construct additional kingdoms into which they could put various groupings of life. The most recent trend in classification has been toward five kingdoms to classify all living things on Earth. Shown here are four kingdoms that—with the animal kingdom—make up a five-kingdom classification structure.

The four kingdoms shown here are the kingdom plantae (mosses, ferns, seed/flowering plants, and other minor groups), kingdom fungi (mushrooms and molds), kingdom protista (algae and protozoa), and kingdom monera (blue-green algae and bacteria). In any kingdom the hierarchy of classification is the same. As this chart shows, groupings go from the most general categories down to the more specific. The most general grouping shown here is PHYLUM (or DIVISION for plants). The most specific grouping listed is ORDER. To use the chart, you may want to find a familiar organism in a CLASS or ORDER box and then trace its classification upward until you reach its PHYLUM or DIVISION.

Schizophyta BACTERIA, BLUE-GREEN ALGAE

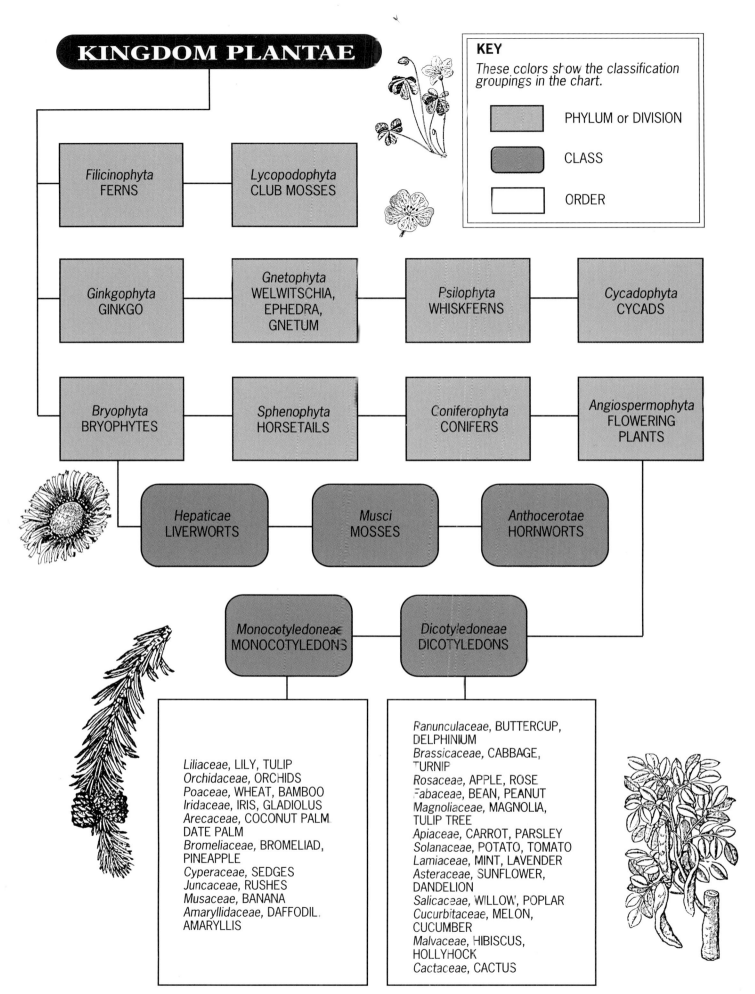

KINGDOM PLANTAE

KEY

These colors show the classification groupings in the chart.

PHYLUM or DIVISION

CLASS

ORDER

Filicinophyta FERNS

Lycopodophyta CLUB MOSSES

Ginkgophyta GINKGO

Gnetophyta WELWITSCHIA, EPHEDRA, GNETUM

Psilophyta WHISKFERNS

Cycadophyta CYCADS

Bryophyta BRYOPHYTES

Sphenophyta HORSETAILS

Coniferophyta CONIFERS

Angiospermophyta FLOWERING PLANTS

Hepaticae LIVERWORTS

Musci MOSSES

Anthocerotae HORNWORTS

Monocotyledoneae MONOCOTYLEDONS

Dicotyledoneae DICOTYLEDONS

Liliaceae, LILY, TULIP
Orchidaceae, ORCHIDS
Poaceae, WHEAT, BAMBOO
Iridaceae, IRIS, GLADIOLUS
Arecaceae, COCONUT PALM, DATE PALM
Bromeliaceae, BROMELIAD, PINEAPPLE
Cyperaceae, SEDGES
Juncaceae, RUSHES
Musaceae, BANANA
Amaryllidaceae, DAFFODIL, AMARYLLIS

Ranunculaceae, BUTTERCUP, DELPHINIUM
Brassicaceae, CABBAGE, TURNIP
Rosaceae, APPLE, ROSE
Fabaceae, BEAN, PEANUT
Magnoliaceae, MAGNOLIA, TULIP TREE
Apiaceae, CARROT, PARSLEY
Solanaceae, POTATO, TOMATO
Lamiaceae, MINT, LAVENDER
Asteraceae, SUNFLOWER, DANDELION
Salicaceae, WILLOW, POPLAR
Cucurbitaceae, MELON, CUCUMBER
Malvaceae, HIBISCUS, HOLLYHOCK
Cactaceae, CACTUS

Glossary

budding A type of asexual reproduction, found in yeasts, in which a small bud that forms on the parent gradually grows into a new organism.

cells Microscopic units that are the building blocks of living things.

consumer An organism that eats other organisms.

decomposer An organism that breaks down dead organisms and waste materials produced by living things.

digestion The mechanical and chemical breakdown of food into substances the body can use for growth and energy.

dormant Inactive, or resting.

environment All the surroundings of an organism.

evolve Change over a long period of time.

excretion The removal of bodily wastes.

extinct No longer in existence.

fermentation A form of respiration that does not require oxygen.

flagella Tail-like appendages on certain fungus spores and one-celled organisms.

food chain The order in which organisms feed on one another in an ecosystem.

fossils Preserved remains or traces of once-living things.

fruiting body The part of a fungus that produces spores.

fungicides Poisonous chemicals used by humans to kill fungus pests.

germination The sprouting of a spore, seed, or other reproductive body.

gills Thin structures on the underside of the caps of many kinds of mushrooms, on which spores are produced.

habitat The place where an organism lives.

hormones Chemicals produced by an organism that regulate various life processes.

host The plant or animal on which a parasite, such as a parasitic fungus, lives.

hyphae Microscopic thread-like structures that make up the bodies of most kinds of fungi.

life cycle All the stages that an organism passes through during its lifetime.

metabolism The chemical processes in cells that are essential to life.

mycelium The tangled mass of hyphae that make up the body of most kinds of fungi.

parasite An organism that lives in or on the body of another organism and gets its food from its host.

producer An organism that makes food.

protoplasm The jelly-like contents of all living cells.

reproduction The process by which organisms create other members of their species.

respiration The process by which organisms get energy from food.

rhizomorph A tough root-like structure, made up of many closely packed fungus hyphae, that can spread over long distances.

saprophyte An organism that feeds on the dead remains of plants and animals.

species A group of organisms that share many traits with one another and that can reproduce with one another.

sporangium A spore container.

spore A reproductive structure, usually one-celled, produced by fungi and certain other organisms, that can develop into a new organism.

stimulus A change in the environment that causes a reaction in an organism.

For Further Reading

Arnosky, Jim. *In the Forest.* New York: Lothrop, Lee & Shepard Books, 1989.

Bailey, Donna. *Forests.* Madison, NJ: Raintree Steck-Vaughn, 1990.

Challand, Helen. *Vanishing Forests.* Chicago: Childrens Press, 1991.

Coil, Suzanne M. *Poisonous Plants.* New York: Franklin Watts, 1991.

Gattis, L.S., III. *Fungi for Pathfinders: A Basic Youth Enrichment Skill Honor Packet.* Antamonte Springs, FL: Cheetah Publishing, 1987.

Greenway, Shirley. *Forests.* Brookfield, CT: Newington, 1991.

Greenaway, Theresa. *First Plants.* Madison, NJ: Raintree Steck-Vaughn, 1990.

Johnson, Sylvia A. *Mushrooms.* Minneapolis, MN: Lerner Publications, 1982.

Kaye, Judith. *The Life of Alexander Fleming.* New York: Twenty-First Century Books, 1992.

Madgwick, Wendy. *Fungi & Lichens.* Madison, NJ: Raintree Steck-Vaughn, 1990.

Peissel, Michel and Allen, Missy. *Dangerous Plants & Mushrooms.* New York: Chelsea House, 1993.

Schwartz, David M. *The Hidden Life of the Forest.* New York: Crown Books for Young Readers, 1988.

Tesar, Jenny E. *Shrinking Forests.* New York: Facts On File, 1991.

Whipple, Jane B. *Forest Resources.* New York: Franklin Watts, 1985.

Index